MY LINES
(An introduction to my poetry)

Written by
Colin Boynton

Dedicated to
Renee Allington – a sadly missed, dear friend.

ISBN : 978-0-9559931-0-7

Best wishes

[signature]

POETRY INDEX

1. MY LINES
2. THE SHADOW OF EVIL
3. TOMORROW
4. SLOW DOWN
5. NOT NOW
6. THE COACH TOUR
7. JANUARY SALES
8. NONSENSE
9. ANOTHER LONELY YEAR
10. LIFE BEGINS AT...?
11. CLOUDS
12. GOING BACK
13. TROUBLES
14. UNTITLED
15. DON'T TAKE LOVE FOR GRANTED
16. FRED
17. THOUGHTS
18. HOPEFUL PARTING
19. CONFESSION
20. PLEASE DON'T SAY GOODBYE
21. HAPPY TIMES
22. NO NAME
23. FULL MOON MADNESS
24. WHO'S FOOLING WHO?
25. GREETINGS

26. UNDER FIRE
27. THE SORROWFUL CRY
28. THE MODERN WORKING LIFE
29. THE LETTER
30. THERE RIGHT BEHIND ME
31. UNTITLED 2
32. MAGIC
33. YOU AND I
34. POETRY IN MOTION
35. A GENTLE LIFT
36. TOGETHER
37. GA GA !!!
38. MR PIANO PLAYER
39. BLOSSOMING FANTASY
40. JUST A LITTLE LOVING
41. WISHES AND DREAMS
42. SUMMER
43. PEOPLE – OF ALL SHAPES (AND SIZES)
44. WINTER WHITE
45. I LOVE YOU
46. PICTURES..PHOTOGRAPHS…
47. JUST A THOUGHT
48. A TRUE FRIEND
49. THE MIDNIGHT THIEF
50. UNTITLED 3.

51. PAST AND GONE
52. A FIGMENT OF MY IMAGINATION
53. JUST THE SAME
54. AFTERNOON TEA
55. 21ST CENTURY MAN
56. TWIGHLIGHT
57. HOME FROM HOME
58. A FOOL SUCH AS I
59. JUST OUT THERE
60. HERE TODAY , GONE TOMORROW
61. LADY…/…AND THE TRAMP
62. TIME
63. WHAT'S IT ALL ABOUT
64. THE MEANING
65. MEMORY LANE
66. OBLIVIOUS AND NUMB
67. I AM STRONG
68. IS ANYONE OUT THERE?
69. SAD MEMORIES
70. AMY
71. NOTHING MUCH AT ALL
72. AIN'T NO CURE
73. GRAND-PRIX
74. UNTITLED 4.
75. TWO LIVES

76. THE TRAVELLERS PRAYER
77. ONE MILLION KISSES
78. GOLDEN DAYS
79. BUTTERFLY
80. WILD FLOWER
81. I PRAY
82. LITTLE BIRD
83. HE WHO HATH NO SUNBED (FOR FRANK)
84. HOMECOMING
85. LOST AMONG THE TEARS
86. KEEPER OF MY HEART
87. FOR YOU
88. ON AND ON
89. TELL ME
90. A NIGHT AT HOME
91. DIVINE INTERVENTION
92. MEMORIES ARE MADE OF THIS 1.
93. MEMORIES ARE MADE OF THIS 2.
94. MEMORIES ARE MADE OF THIS 3.
95. YOU
96. LEFT ALL ON HER OWN
97. THAT SINKING FEELING
98. (THE GREAT) ESCAPE
99. LUNCHTIME(REVENGE)
100.   BEN

1. MY LINES.
An introduction to my poetry

Don't ask me to interpret
Something I don't know,
All I do is sit here
And slowly watch it grow.
I don't know where it comes from,
It just seems to appear,
Quickly line by line by line
And then my poem's here.
I have no time to stop and think
What I write about,
The words just flow into my mind
I have to let them out.
Don't ask me to interpret
I can't even explain,
The words just make a poem
Time and time again.

2. THE SHADOW OF EVIL

For all those souls who die in fear
May you find peace at last,
No more to run, no more to hide
Your hurting now be past,
And as the terror spreads it's wings
And flies across the land,
Those of you who wait with tears
Can only watch and stand,
Not knowing where the shadow is
Or where it next may call,
Together standing side by side
Together standing tall,
All as one in grief and pain
Yet feeling all alone,
The whole world watches on in shock
For those not going home,
Tomorrow is another day
One we all must face,
Not knowing what the future brings
For the human race,
Together we must stand up
Strong and proud and tall,
Fighting back together
Until the shadows fall,
And when at last that day is here
When the world is free,
No more souls need die in fear
Perhaps we all will see,
That all it really takes is love
And just a little care,
To live our lives in harmony
The world is ours to share.

3. TOMORROW

In the early morning sunrise
The clouds begin to part
If only they could take away
The pain here in my heart.
I stand here and I look out
Across a field of green
Looking for a figure
That still remains unseen.
I look out here at midday
The sun is shining bright
I find my eyes are blinded
By the very light.
And still I see no figure
There's no one drawing near
I find I skip a heartbeat
In terror and in fear.
The sky has turned to orange
The sun begun to set
I see a shadow reaching out
I cannot reach it yet.
I close my eyes and tremble
The shadows drawing near
And very soon I realise
There's nothing left to fear.
I wait a little longer
The shadow passes by
And moves into the darkness
I hear a gentle sigh.
I close my eyes a moment
Then turn and walk away
The tear that rolls down on my cheek
Will fall another day.

4. SLOW DOWN

What's the point in rushing ?
Time goes by too fast,
No sooner has the day begun
When soon the day is past.
Take some time in what you do
Enjoy the world around
Take a look at life about
Listen to each sound.
Your world will seem a different place
Wonderous and new
Your life will feel much richer
With everything you do.

5. NOT NOW.

He wandered lonely as a cloud
But that was long ago
With all the cloud that's up there now
The sky's as white as snow
He wouldn't feel as lonely
In amongst that crowd
He couldn't even wander now
Lonely as a cloud.

6. THE COACH TOUR (or Sightseeing, Not Half!)

"Eyes all to the left please
Eyes all to the right"
And still the coach still trundled on
Past another sight.
"This is where the hero lived
And this is where he died"
Still they hardly get to see
No matter how they tried.
"There's another site folks
Something else to see,
Got to keep on moving
It's almost half past three.
We haven't time for photographs
There's still a lot to do
I know I shouldn't let you stop
At just turned half past two."
"Eyes to the left please
Eyes all to the right
We have a lot more things to see
Before day turns to night."
"You have to see the sights folks
So please do as I say
I've got my list to follow
Each and every day.
I mustn't miss a thing out
You have to see it all
And here we are last please
Our final port of call.
We haven't time for photographs
We have to get on back
Don't get off the coach please
You'll all get me the sack.
Do get on the coach please
Where are you going to ?
Don't get on the train there
You don't know what to do.
Please get on the coach folks
Do not wave goodbye
I try to do my job well
Honestly – I try."

7. JANUARY SALES

Christmas came and Christmas went
With all our money nearly spent,
Once again the sales are here
How I hate this time of year.
Spend, spend, spend, is all we do
The debts all mount up, worries too,
Bargains all have such appeal
A price like that is now a steal.
I shouldn't let the chance go by
I queued all night so I could buy,
The credit card is now my friend
But will this spending ever end?
Up and up the debts soon mount
And by day three I've then lost count.
Do I care or do I mind
Another bargain I then find.
The debts still mounting one by one
Now my money is all gone,
A panic starts I'm in a sweat
There's loads more bargains I could get.
With no more money left to spend
It feels just like my life will end,
What to do or where to go
To hide from bargains now on show.
How I hate this time of year
I end up living in such fear,
The craving grows once it gets hold
I cannot stop 'til all is sold,
I wish I could just hibernate
And miss this time of year I hate.

8. NONSENSE

Last night as I lay sitting
Beside the open fire
I watched the embers dying
As the flames became much higher
I ate my cup of coffee
And drank a piece of cake
My snoring got much louder
Keeping me awake
The light was getting darker
The sun was shining bright
The midday heat was scorching
In the middle of the night
The time had come to go to bed
And so I closed the door
Climbed the stairs one by one
Until I found the floor
The grass was needing cutting
Underneath the bed
I closed my eyes and went to sleep
And ate my jam and bread.

9. ANOTHER LONELY YEAR

As I sit here watching
The slowly setting sun
The shadows grow much longer
When the day is done,
The air becomes much colder
As night is drawing near
I feel a sadness growing
And shed a single tear.
I sit here and I wonder
Whilst I am all alone
Another year will soon begin
Where has the old one gone?
They seem to pass so quickly
Now that I am old
And no one seems to notice
The sadness that I hold.
And as the days pass quickly by
The new year in the past
Everyone then soon forgets
Very, very fast,
The loneliness that one can feel
Even in a crowd,
Even when you're smiling
Or laughing out aloud.
I'll sit here and remember
Things from out my past
Things that made me happy
I'm glad that memories last,
I hope I never lose them
I hope they'll always stay
I know they'll bring me lot's of joy
On a lonely day.

10. LIFE BEGINS AT…?

More so them the fool than I
Who want to sit around and sigh,
They'll sit and wait for life to start
Waiting with an aching heart,
But life will only really start
When you decide to take your part,
Don't just sit there asking why?
Or life will simply pass you by.

11. CLOUDS

I see the clouds are passing by
Making patterns in the sky
It only really caught my eye
When I saw a butterfly.

They look so fluffy and so white
When the sun is shining bright
And even in the dead of night
You'll see them in the full moon light.

They change so quickly one by one
Before you know it, they are gone
Drifting past the midday sun
Watching clouds can be such fun.

12. GOING BACK

Last night I took another step
Forwards to my past,
Reliving some more memories
I never thought would last,
I still could hear the laughter,
And all the many cries,
Lot's of happy greetings,
Lot's of sad goodbyes,
You know there's no escaping
You cannot run and hide,
They're with you for a lifetime
In front, behind, beside.

13. TROUBLES

You've got your troubles
I have got mine
If we got together
Would things work out fine?
If things worked out fine
For you and for me
Think how much happier
We both could be,
And if we were happy
We'd share our good news,
And tell the whole world
What it needs to do,
The world has it's troubles
I have got mine,
Perhaps one day
All will be fine.

14. UNTITLED

There's a petal from a flower
Lying on the floor,
Blown around in circles
By a draft below the door,
It lost it's scent and came to rest
Lying on the floor,
And soon that little petal
Was joined by just one more.

15. DON'T TAKE LOVE FOR GRANTED

I shouldn't take for granted
The love you give to me,
Although it's very difficult
The reason is you see,
Sometimes when I am lonely
And have nowhere to go,
And have no one to talk to
When I'm feeling low,
I only have to stop and think
Remind myself of you,
I feel your love surround me
And lift my spirits too,
It doesn't matter where I am
Or even what I do,
I know your love will reach me
My love,
I love you too.

16. FRED.

I have a little spider,
My spiders name is Fred,
But I really don't like spiders
And sometimes wish them dead.
I do not want to squash them,
Or splat them to the wall
And if I see them hanging down
I'm frightened they might fall.
I never have liked spiders,
But really love my Fred,
You would love him also,
If he shared your bed!

17. THOUGHTS

Walking through a graveyard
On a winter afternoon,
The dying light reflecting
All the misery and gloom.
A layer of snow is hiding
All the footsteps out of sight,
And all too soon the world
Will be hidden by the night.
Reading names and sentiments
From ages now long gone,
Makes us stop to think about
The things that's yet to come.
A fleeting shadow from the past
A fading memory,
Of people, places that you knew
Or things that used to be.
And as you leave and close the gate
You leave those thoughts behind
Hidden in a cemetery
Buried in your mind.

18. HOPEFUL PARTING

And as my friend
We say goodbye,
I know we'll meet again,
In a little meadow
Or down a country lane.
I know that I will miss you
Throughout the days to come,
So hurry chase the dark clouds,
You are my friend the sun.

19. CONFESSION

I have a little secret,
Something to confess,
I've had it for a long time now
And I'm getting in a mess.
It creeps up from behind me
I cannot shake it off,
I am a chocaholic
And cannot get enough.

20. PLEASE DON'T SAY GOODBYE

Through the window at the far side
We could see the setting sun,
You seemed to grow more restful
And knew your time had come.
It seemed to be so easy
For you to say goodbye,
Whilst we were left here all alone
We asked each other – why ?

21. HAPPY TIMES

Grey hair
No teeth
Wrinkled stockings
Round her feet.
All smiles
Mind long gone
She walks around
And sings a song.
In a world
That's all her own
In a home
That's not her home.
Pity those
Who cannot see
Just how happy
She can be.

22. NO NAME

Walking down a darkened street,
Dancing leaves around my feet,
Falling raindrops on my head,
I wonder where to make my bed?
Feeling free, but all alone
Wishing that I had a home.
Walking parks at dead of night,
I keep myself well out of sight.
Moving on at break of day,
Afraid of what most people say.
And every day is just the same,
For a man who has no name.

23. FULL MOON MADNESS

Last night as you lay sleeping
I crept out of the room,
Down into the garden
To howl at the full moon.
My shaggy coat became dark grey,
My paws began to form,
I rolled about upon my back
Across my own front lawn.
I really hate this time of month
It makes me feel quite queer,
'Cause whilst I am a werewolf
I just go right off beer.

24. WHO'S FOOLING WHO ?

A biscuit and a piece of cake
Early morning teas,
It doesn't seem to matter
When you're counting calories.
This one doesn't really count,
I'm sure it will not show,
Just this little extra bit,
Who is going to know?
Excuse follows excuse,
And pound will follow pound,
Why this diet doesn't work,
I cannot understand.

25. GREETINGS !

A picture postcard came today
A pretty scene from far away,
Sent by friends from overseas
Far away on holidays.
"Lovely views – weather fine
Must come back another time,
Seen many things, many places
Met some old friends – and new faces."
A picture postcard came today
From friends who'd been on holiday.
It took it's time in getting here,
They got back, late last year!

26. UNDER FIRE

Someone told me yesterday
Some very strange odd news,
And yesterday they chattered
In the supermarket queues,
Had I really done that ?
I just do not recall
I don't even remember
If I was there at all.
You know what gossip mongers are
Once they think they know,
No matter if it's true or false
They don't accept your "NO"
They'll talk about you all the time
Although you've done no wrong
Then talk about somebody else
When gossip comes along.

27. THE SORROWFUL CRY

And the earth cried out for salvation
"Please help me if you can,
You're destroying the trees and the flowers,
And even your fellow man.
Stop the things you are doing,
Polluting the land and your mind,
Don't you see what you're doing?
Are you so deaf and so blind?"

And still the earth keeps on turning,
Day follows night follows day,
But for some poor soul who was living
His life has been taken away.
No one asked his opinion,
Or asked him what he would do,
They all just kept on fighting
T'was all they ever knew.

And soon the cries for salvation
Will be carried away on a breeze,
No one to hear what you're saying
Drifting around the dead trees.
The sun will still rise in the morning,
The clouds will just roll on by,
And the world just keeps on turning
Until the day it must die.

And no one will hear what is happening,
There'll be no one left to see,
Destroyed by one another
Instead of just letting be.
Our cries of death and destruction
Will fade as the years pass on by,
And no one will hear at the end
Earths last sorrowful cry

28. THE MODERN WORKING LIFE

It seems to me,
That you're living a life,
That is always full
Of trouble and strife,
Rushing around
To get things done,
Living your life
On the run,
Living your life
At break neck pace,
Is this what you call
The new rat race?
Is this what you call
Living a life?
Then I'd rather step back
From this trouble and strife.

29. THE LETTER

Isn't it funny,
Isn't it queer,
Getting this restless
When you get near,
Isn't it odd,
Isn't it strange,
Feeling like this
When you're within range,
I know it will happen
Time and again,
It's getting to be
A bit of a pain,
At my time of life,
I ought to know better,
Instead I just sit down
And write out the letter,
"Dear Santa Claus
Now Christmas is near,
Here are a few things
That I'd like this year"

30. THERE RIGHT BEHIND ME

Whenever I walk
Back down this street,
I hear the sound
Of somebody's feet,
Following me
As I walk along,
I turn to look back
And find they have gone,
I hear their laughter
Coming quite clear,
From somewhere behind me
And yet very near.
I turn to look back,
There's no one around,
And yet I heard clearly
That loud merry sound.
Could it just be
That the things that I hear,
Are sounds of my memories
Loud in my ear?

31. UNTITLED . 2.

Away you flew
One moonlit night
While all the world
Was hid from sight
Where you went to
No one knows
Could it be
Where warm wind blows?
You went away
With no farewell
Why you went
You didn't tell
You just came back
One bright day
As though you'd never
Been away
Where you went
What you did
No one knows
You never said.

32. MAGIC

Rainbow dreams and wishes
A magic carpet ride
Fairies in the garden
A sweet young princess bride
The innocence of childhood
All too quickly gone
Passed through generations
The magic carries on.

33. YOU AND I

I look at you
You look at me
Do you see
What others see?
You search my face
And look inside
My inner thoughts
I cannot hide.
You've seen me oft
And know me well
What you think
Who can tell?
I look at you
You look at me
In the mirror
  - Imagery.
I lool at you
You look at me
We two are one
Eternally.

34. POETRY IN MOTION

From the early morning
Across the waking land
Until the fall of night time
When darkness will descend.
Birds that fly above the trees
Fish deep in an ocean
A breeze that stirs a tiny flower
It's poetry in motion.
The whisper of the raindrops
That fall upon the land
A bee upon a flower
A wave upon the sand.
Behind a drifting cloud
A fleeting glimpse of sun
On poetry in motion
Until the day is done.

35. A GENTLE LIFT

I've gazed upon the distant hills
Looked down on valleys low
Walked through fields
Crossed over streams
And watched a river flow.

I've wandered in and out through trees
Through forests and through woods
Felt the sun
Upon my face
That lifts my dullest moods.

I've travelled far in distant lands
And seen a many thing
It's all of nature everywhere
That makes
My poor heart sing.

36. TOGETHER

The rain may damp my spirit
But stars will light my soul,
While moonlight casts a shadow
On days that take their toll,
I take my life within my hands
Your love deep in my heart,
And walk along life's troubled path
Knowing we wont part.

37. GA GA !!!

I tiddely I toe
Iddely piddely pum
Inky pinky poo poo
Widely tiddely tum !!!

38. MR PIANO PLAYER

Tinkle tinkle
Piano player
Tuneful you may be
Each time you play
A little tune
Flat is middle C!

Tinkle tinkle
On the keys
Playing every day
Each melody's
Made different
In some strange kind of way!!

Tinkle tinkle
Piano player
Perhaps it just might be
Each melody
Sounds different
'Cause flat is middle C!!!

Tinkle tinkle
On the keys
I know your name is Geoff
Those awful tunes
Don't bother you
Because you are stone deaf!!!!

39. BLOSSOMING FANTASY

Shall we dance in the sunshine
To-day my dear
Or just watch the clouds passing by
Feel the breeze
Brush our face
In the shade of the tree
Watch the birds and the butterfly.

What a life that we lead
As we grow from the seed
Not a trouble, a worry
A care
Nothing to do
Except please you
As you come
And you stop, and you stare.

Shall we dance in the sunshine
To-day my dear
And wait for an April shower
What a life that we lead
As we grow from the seed
I'm glad that I'm only
A flower!

40. JUST A LITTLE LOVING

I've watched the world
So many times
And much has passed on through.
Some people paused
Some people stayed
Each time I never knew.
Surrounded by our private worlds
Each and every one
I never even gave a thought
Until the time had gone.
We're all so very singular
Private in our ways
Yet all together in this world
Throughout our lifelong days.
It really is no wonder
The world is what it is
We've little time to give each other
Let's get back what there was.
So try and show a little love
As we go along our way
The world might get a better place
Slowy
Day
By
Day.

41. WISHES AND DREAMS

Close your eyes
And wish upon
The star that shines above
In a dream
All alone
Or with the one you love.

Like magic
Found in fairytales
That cast a spell on you
In a dream
Your wishes
You know can all come true.

Our lives
They rush so quickly by
Our dreams
Too soon are gone
And all that's left
Are memories
That linger on and on.

So live your dreams
And hold your wish
Don't ever let them die
For at the end
They don't go on
Beside you
They must lie.

42. SUMMER

Oh to be in sunshine
Get out of this cold rain
How I long for winter
Now summer's here again.

Oh to see a snowflake
Or feel a frosty morn'
How I long for winter
And wish the summer gone.

Oh to be in sunshine
To have some heat and light
How I long for winter
For weather that's just right!

43. PEOPLE – OF ALL SHAPES (AND SIZES)

Tubby, fat or thin
Be they young or old
The shapes they all come in
Vary many fold.

Be they men or women
They might be short or tall
The clothes that they all fill in
Range from big to small.

People can amuse me
Bodies can amaze
It depends on how I see them
Or even hold a gaze.

It's not what's on the outside
But really what's within
The bodies that we all hide
Tubby, fat or thin.

44. WINTER WHITE

A creeping veil, a shroud of white
Slowly hiding all from sight,
Frosted branches, dust of ice
Peeping out to fool our eyes.
And gently, gently the world slows down
Day passes by, night comes around.
The air is still and all is calm
Waiting for the day to warm.
A warmth that never seems to come
Not even with the midday sun.
Then once again the veil of white
Begins to hide the world from sight.

45. I LOVE YOU

"I love You"
Seems too simple
"I love you "
Seems too small,
But,
"I love you"
Are three simple words
That seem to say it all.

46. PICTURES...PHOTOGRAPHS...

A picture,
A photograph,
Memories that make us laugh
Reminders, which also make us cry.
An object,
A token,
Tells of hearts broken,
Reminders, which also make us sigh.
Some pieces,
Some treasure,
Bringers of great pleasure
Reminders, which helps the day go by.
Pictures,
Photographs,
Memories of days gone past,
Remind us
They'll never die.

47. JUST A THOUGHT

I look up to the sky at night
And see the stars
That shine so bright
And wonder to myself
"Which one is yours?"

48. A TRUE FRIEND

As mysteries of life unfold
I've seen so many things
And met so many people
I like what life can bring,
Mother nature – one good friend
With me every day
Never seems to let me down
Beside me all the way.
And if perchance I may forget
My heart, my mind be down
I'm soon made bright and cheery
By looking all around.
So if sometime you're down at heart
Please call upon my friend
She's always there to take the part
And make your sorrow end.

49. THE MIDNIGHT THEIF

It was there last night, whole, complete,
Not a crumb was out of place,
It's now half gone in just one night
Who could have filled their face?
With cream to ooze out of the sides
A nice thick layer of jam,
Sitting on the middle shelf
Beside the piece of ham.
And that has lost a slice or two
Someone had a feast
It seems there is a thief about
Is it man or beast?
Could I be mistaken,
Or is it really true,
Instead of four jam doughnuts
We're only left with two.
Their teeth will rot, of that I'm sure
It serves them right no doubt,
And if I catch the culprit
The rest will soon come out.
I'm sorry dear, what did you say?
I sleep walk every night
In fact I woke you up before
And gave you such a fright.
For down the stairs along the hall
The kitchen door was shut,
You peeped on through
And saw the fridge was where my head was put.
Eating of the cream cake
Having eaten ham,
And holding in my other hand
Two doughnuts filled with jam!

50. UNTITLED 3.

If the sun could dry away
The tears of the world
Crying all would be in vain
And petals stay unfurled.
But as there's tear drops falling
As heavy as the rain,
Little flowers blossom
And take away our pain.
We know that God is watching down
Taking care of us,
By showing us the beauty
In everything he does.
Reminding each and everyone
Though things might seem quite sad
Nothing is unbearable
And nothing is that bad.

51. PAST AND GONE

Why do we lose
The ones we love?
And should I believe
In God above?
Why all the suffering
Why all the pain?
And will the love
Come back again?
I can't turn back
The hands of time,
I'll make the most
Of what is mine.
Tomorrow
Quickly marches on
Today becomes yesterday
Is gone.

52. A FIGMENT OF MY IMAGINATION

Every day
I'm looking upon
Something quite strange
That's short fat and long.
But don't ask me what
It is that I see
But sometimes I find
It's looking at me.
It never moves round
It just sits right there
Looking as if
It hasn't a care.
No one else notices
No one else sees
You'd think that this thing
Was hid in the trees.
I'm frightened to think
One day I will find
This strange little thing
Is just in my mind!

53. JUST THE SAME

The anger and the hatred
The bitter twistedness
Could this be the reason
The world is in a mess?
And could there be a reason
Why people feel this way?
It seems it's only getting worse
With every passing day
What happened to the feeling
Your neighbour was your friend,
What happened in our lifetime
To make these feelings end?
Can we ever get back
The spirit and the joy?
Like in the days of long ago
When I was just a boy.
Or do I now remember
Things quite differently?
And have these things now really changed
From how they used to be?

54. AFTERNOON TEA

Someone cried "Smile!" and we all did,
My, what a sight that must be
Us toothless old wrinklies all hunched together
Having our afternoon tea.
Crumbs on the table, and down on the floor
It cannot be helped you see,
They fall through the gaps that we have in our mouths
The one's where our teeth used to be.
There's puddles of tea in our saucers
And dribbles have run down our chin
And if they'd put something into our cups,
Just think of the mess we'd be in.
We come here each Wednesday P.M.
To partake of our afternoon tea,
But today is a special occasion
Old Tom is 100 you see!

55. 21st CENTURY MAN

In a world full of violence
We're stunned by the silence
Of voices we've never heard,
It's the cry in the dark
That ignites the spark
Pleading that something be done.
Ignoring each other
Like sister and brother
Who knows if we really cared,
It's the battles we fight
Hidden from sight
That are never really won.
We live out our lives
As husbands and wives
Going our own separate ways
Eyes shut tight
To the horrible sight
Of the death and destruction about.
From out of the past
It happens so fast
We head to the end of our days,
And once we are gone
Mankind will go on
The same as before no doubt.

56. TWIGHLIGHT

In the light of an early summers eve
By the side of a slow flowing stream,
Is where the old man likes to sit
And watch, and wait, and dream.
Of times that are past in the long gone years
And all the things he has done,
Now in the twighlight of his years
He watches the setting sun,
As it slowly sinks beyond distant hills
A chill soon fills the air,
And shivers run up and down his back
From a ghost from his past that is there,
Haunting him like some strange melody
It swirls around in his head,
Memories of people and friends that he knew
All of them now long dead,
Buried there in the cemetery
On the other side of the stream
Where the old man likes to sit each day
To watch, and wait, and dream.

57. HOME FROM HOME

Underneath the arches
The wind blows hard and cold,
Litter piles up all around
New upon the old.
Hidden in a corner
The old man huddles down,
Covered up with boxes
He finds about the town.
The morning papers keep him warm
Tucked below his things,
The evening paper lines his shoes
His trousers tied with strings.
Each day passes into weeks
Years keep passing by,
Time it has no meaning now
He's waiting just to die,
What a sad and lonely end
For such a long lived life,
To end up living on the streets
No children and no wife.
And people pass him every day
No one seems to care,
A glance is all they give him
They leave him lying there.
Underneath the arches
A story now is told,
Of litter now piled on top
A body still and cold.

58. A FOOL SUCH AS I

I wandered through the rain last night,
And my, I looked an awful sight,
Rain drenched clothes and rain drenched hair,
I really shouldn't have been out there.
My death of cold I'll catch one day,
For walking out in such a way.
The fool am I and such a twit
For wanting out a little bit,
The fool am I for giving way
The dog first walked – then ran away.
I looked around, I gave a shout,
And though 'twas raining, I stayed out.
"Poor soul he's lost, where could he be?"
This thought and more, it worried me.
Midnight came, midnight went,
One o'clock, I'm not content.
Two o'clock and still no sign
And soaking wet I draw the line.
Feeling blue and feeling low,
I went back home – where could I go?
My dearest pal and lifelong friend,
Was this how it was to end?
I pushed the door, it opened wide,
And that damn dog was sat inside.
Keeping dry and keeping warm,
And keeping well away from harm.
And though I'm tired and soaking through,
I love that dog –
He loves me too!

59. JUST OUT THERE

There's every shade of rainbow
Growing just out there,
And every scent of flower
Is drifting on the air.
It greets me every morning
Until the evening light
I cannot help but be amazed
At such a wondrous sight.
And every turn I make through life
I see it everywhere
And every road I go along
I know I'll find it there.
Everyone can find it,
Not everyone will see
They seem to be quite blind at times
They only think of "me."
If only they would stop a while
And take a look around
The beauty of the world is on
The sky, the sea, the ground.

60. HERE TODAY, GONE TOMORROW

Last night as I was sitting
By the dying fire light
A little moth just caught my eye
Then vanished out of sight.
There for just a minute
Then disappeared from view
It made me stop and realise
My life is like that too.
That minute is my lifetime
Too quickly passing by,
In the measure of eternity
The blinking of an eye.

61. LADY...

It's just an old familiar face
That no one seems to see,
She travelled round the city streets
No dreams of what could be.
Carrying her worldly goods
In two old shopping bags,
She'd had them for a long time now
Both found, stuffed with rags.
Tatty clothes and worn out shoes
Hair all in a mess,
She went to church each Sunday
To go to weekly mass.
She never had an ounce of gold,
And never saw the glitter,
Her old and worn out broken body
Lies among the litter.
No one cares, nor seems to see
Rushing on their way,
A former life that used to be
Now past her final day.

...AND THE TRAMP

I do not want to notice,
I do not want to see,
The beggar sat upon the street,
Pleading out to me.
"Spare some money for us,
Just a cup of tea!"
Remember for the grace of God,
That beggar could be me.

62. TIME

There's a very old grandfather clock
Standing in the hall,
It's face is to the future
It's back against the wall.
The hands of time keep sweeping round
The face upon the clock,
The swinging of the pendulum
A gentle tick and tock.
Father time keeps marching through
Mother natures world,
Our history that's now long past,
Are stories being told.
The future rushes on us
Too soon becomes the past,
And as we grow much older
Time seems to go too fast.
Yet time means very little
To that clock stood in the hall,
It only has to mark out time,
Passing for us all.

63. WHAT'S IT ALL ABOUT

Going through a lifetime
Changing day to day,
And picking up the pieces
You dropped along the way.
Storing up the memories
And things you never need,
Falling down on hard times
Doesn't mean we bleed.
Life is just a mystery
Does it make much sense?
Most of us don't even try
We just sit on the fence.
Does it really matter,
For in the end we find,
Much of all the mystery
We're going to leave behind.

64. THE MEANING

A love that's tender
One that's rare
A love we two were meant to share,
I need you
As you need me
Our being together was meant to be,
So I found love
One that's true
A love that's meant to be with you,
I found love
That's going to last
That means my lonely days are past.
I love you
And you love me
Together – until eternity.

65. MEMORY LANE

I walked back down the street last night
To be with you again,
The street that has no city
The street that has no name,
And still it's very busy
When I'm down memory lane.

I step outside my doorway
Just to be with you,
Go for walks down country lanes
The way we used to do.
I still can hear your laughter
Your voice is everywhere
Just to see your face again
Just to touch your hair.

I walked back down the street last night
To be with you again,
The street was very busy,
And still I call your name.
Do you ever hear me
When I'm down memory lane?

I slowly start to wander
Where my mind will let me go,
Reliving many memories
Of all I used to know.
Some of them will bring a smile
Others bring a tear,
And still I hold on to the dream
To have you once more near.

I'm walking down the street again
I cannot keep away,
It holds for me sweet memories
I live them day to day,
And though some days it brings me joy
Some days it brings me pain,
I know I'll always want to walk
My way down memory lane.

66. OBLIVIOUS AND NUMB

We're living in a world of dirt
A city full of sin,
No shame for all the things we've done
Or for the mess we're in.
Litter blows about the streets
Thrown from home and car,
There is no pride in how we live
How did we fall so far?
We seem to need destruction
Violence and pain,
And yet we only have one world,
The chance won't come again.
Will our children love us
In the years to come,
Do you think they'll thank us
For all the things we've done,
Or as they grow and look around
Will they too become
Uncaring and destructive,
Oblivious and numb?

67. I AM STRONG

Green grow the grasses
On both sides of the street,
So why do I see jealousy
In people that I meet?
Why, do they always want
The things that I have now,
They're never even satisfied
And take things anyhow.
They steal away possessions
Try to take my pride,
Try and take my dignity
And leave me on the side.
But I will always rise up
And carry on my way,
I won't let them defeat me
No matter what they say.

68. IS ANYONE OUT THERE?

Won't someone play that melody?
That tune from way back when,
The one you always used to play
Over and again.
Won't someone come and dance with me?
Hold me in their arms,
Put a smile back on my face
Using all their charms.
Won't someone come and talk with me?
I'm feeling all alone,
Sitting in this little room
Here all on my own.
Won't someone come and sit with me?
I'm waiting just to die,
My time has been a happy one
So please don't sit and cry.
Is anybody out there?
Will someone hear my plea?
I just don't want to be alone?
Won't someone – please.

69. SAD MEMORIES

I'm sure that they are watching me
They follow me about,
They're trying just to catch me
Of that I have no doubt.
At night they creep upon me
Haunting all my dreams,
I know I can't escape them
Nothing's as it seems.
There's nowhere left for me to go,
They always find me there,
Coming once more up to me
Whilst sitting in my chair.

70. AMY

There's no one quite like Amy,
The only lady for me,
And wish I could have Amy
To sit upon my knee.
There's no one quite like Amy,
Her smiles are just for me,
And when I go to see her
We share a cup of tea.
There's no one else like Amy,
As sweet as she can be,
I wish she was my girlfriend
But I am only three!

71. NOTHING MUCH AT ALL

With nothing left to hold on to
But a fading memory,
A photograph of me and you
And how things used to be.
There's no one else can know but you
The things that you now see,
There's nothing in the world that's new
And nothing left to be.
You've done the things you wanted to
Been happy and carefree,
There's nothing else that you can do
But grow old gracefully.

72. AIN'T NO CURE!

I'm holding my breath
And counting to ten,
That is when
I hiccup again.
It all began
A few days ago,
And now that it's started
It just won't go.
The pain I am feeling
Deep in my chest,
Hurts so much
I cannot rest.
I haven't slept
Since it began,
I've tried lots of cures
The best I can.
I'm holding my breath
Once again,
And feeling faint
That is when…………………..
…………………………………………………………
……………………………………………………………
…….
……………………………………………………………
……………!

73. GRAND – PRIX

So there I am each morning
Another race begins,
I may not want to enter
And no one ever wins.
We line up at the red light
Waiting for the green,
Then just as it is changing
Some cars just can't be seen.
They race off down the high street
At speeds they shouldn't do,
Who are they impressing?
It isn't me or you.
They disappear so quickly
I've hardly crossed the line,
And then another races past
Yet still I'm doing fine.
We always seem to meet up
At some other place,
So why do they keep speeding?
There is no need to race.
If they keep on driving
The way they always do,
They'll end up hurting someone,
It could be me or you.
As I have to drive each day
I'll do my steady pace,
And try and keep out of the way
Of the daily race.

74. UNTITLED 4.

You wake up every morning
And everythings the same,
Nothing ever seems to change
You wish you had an aim.
A name that you could call yourself
And not be just a face,
Running with the others
In the very same rat race.
You wish you could be different
Not like all the rest,
No matter how you try to change
What they have seems best.
The grass may seem much greener
On the other side,
But every time you cross,
The grass is brown and dried.
So take the things you're given
Just the way they are,
Do not try and change them
As you're better off by far.

75. TWO LIVES

I don't know who they are
Or even where they're from
A cheery smile,
One quick hello
Then slowly amble on.
The look of slight abandonment
Of nowhere to belong
Clothing slightly tattered
Fingers cold and numb.
Always going one way
Never looking back,
One will hold some papers
The other holds a sack.
They seem so very happy
With the life they lead,
Never really wanting
Yet getting what they need.
No burden laden shoulders
Few worries on their mind
As long as they've each other
They'll take things as they find.
How nice to keep life simple
Push daily chores aside,
Just travel through their lives as one
The wanderer and his bride.

76. THE TRAVELLERS PRAYER

As I go my way today
I close my hands and then I pray.
Lord have mercy, Lord be kind
To my loved ones left behind.
And on return at end of day
I close my hands once more and pray,
That all I love are safe and well
And live another day to tell.

77. ONE MILLION KISSES

One million kisses in my heart
Proves my love we'll never part,
Another kiss will overflow
Where my love will that kiss go?
In my soul for all to see
From there into eternity.

78. GOLDEN DAYS

A golden October
A bright sunny day
The gentlest breeze
Sends leaves on their way,
Birds in the treetops
Clouds drifting by
Retreat of the bee
And the last butterfly,
One final outburst
One final fling
Before cold and dark winter days
Then set in.

79. BUTTERFLY

A ripple on the water
Slowly spreads it's rings,
A gentle little butterfly
Slowly spreads it's wings,
Flying in the summer sun
On a gentle breeze,
Flitting round the flowers
In among the trees.
Spreading just a little joy
Beauty on a wing,
To think there's all that beauty
In such a tiny thing.

80. WILDFLOWER

One by one by one by one
Slowly budding then become
The brightest colours ever seen
Sprinkled there amongst the green
Bright and shining,
Bright and new
Brought alive by morning dew.

One by one by one by one
Open in the morning sun,
There for all the world to see
All this glory and beauty
Bright and shining
Bright and new
Missed by many, ignored too.

One by one by one by one
Blooming in the summer sun
It's such a pity such a shame
For every flower has a name
So why can't everybody see
The beauty growing there for me?

81. I PRAY

I pray for you,
I pray for me,
I pray that every day will be,
Full of joy
And good health
Appreciating
The wealth
Of the beauty on this earth
Around us from before our birth,
Around us on the day we die
And when we say our last goodbye.

82. LITTLE BIRD

Oh the joy that there must be,
Flying round from tree to tree,
With no worries and no cares
Of the world today.
Looking down from way up high
In your world up in the sky
Seeing all of mankinds trouble
In the world today.
Flying round on fragile wings
Making music no one sings
Oh such beauty we should see
In the world today.

83. HE WHO HATH NO SUNBED (FOR FRANK)

It's only just turned 6 o'clock
The sun is not yet out,
But looking down around the pool
There's towels all about,
Do these people go to bed
Or are they up all night?
There's another towel
Coming into sight.
They must be very insecure
Up before the sun,
Rushing for a sunbed
Before the last one's gone.
But there's plenty out there
Enough for everyone,
Remember, he who hath no sunbed
He will have no sun.

84. HOMECOMING

The years are upon me
My eyes are grown dim
My heart has been longing
To be home again,
For too many years now
I've been far away
So take me back home now
To where I will stay.
Take me back
To the Highlands my home
Where my heart is uplifted
My spirit can roam
To gaze across waters
Of glistening loch
My eyes will look over
The mountains and rock
So take me back
To the Highlands my home
I'll lay my head down there
No more will I roam.
I've been upon water
And far distant shore
But now that I'm home
I'll travel no more
This place that I love so
This land I call home
The ache in my heart
Whenever I roam.
So take me back
To the highlands my home
Where my heart is uplifted
My spirit can roam
Where my soul is in heaven
I'll find peace at last
Out there in the heather
My life is now past
So take me back
To the highlands my home
And lay me to rest there
No more will I roam.

85. LOST AMONG THE TEARS

I take a look around me
At a world of green and blue
A world so full of colour
That's home for me and you
A world that has destruction
Violence and pain
Through time we keep on wondering
Will peace come back again?
And though the years may come and go
There never seems to be
A time that's truly peaceful
And free of cruelty.
Infliction caused by mankind
On mankind out of hate
We should just stop and take a look
Before it is too late.
Tomorrow is too precious
For some it will not come
And those of us now left behind
There's no where left to run.
Face up to reality
And truth that's hard to bear
See the hatred in a face
Does anybody care?
The world is always crying
Crying out with pain
Hurting from the lack of care
There's only greed and gain.
When will mankind ever learn
The error of their ways
Or will this be the way they choose
To end their living days.
It only takes a little love
And isn't hard to do
Show it for your fellow man
It isn't something new,
It's love that's been forgotten
Neglected through the years
Hidden by the hating
Lost among the tears.

MY LINES

MY FIRST BOOK OF POETRY TITLED "MY LINES"
HAS NOW BEEN PUBLISHED AND
IS AVAILABLE TO PURCHASE AS FOLLOWS:
ONLINE FROM AMAZON OR: www.lulu.com OR
FROM BOOKSHOPS QUOTING ISBN No. :
978-0-9559931-0-7
OR WRITE FOR A PERSONAL SIGNED COPY
ENCLOSING A CHEQUE FOR £8.00 (INC p&p)
TO:
COLIN BOYNTON,
29 RIPON GARDENS,
HARPUR HILL,
BUXTON,
DERBYSHIRE.
SK 17 9PL

Please allow 28 days for delivery of signed copies.

Good better Best :

Never let it rest
until your good is better
and your better best.

Foxton Locks. near Leister.
                    Leicester.

86. KEEPER OF MY HEART

If one day when you awake
You find me lying here
And there's a smile upon my face
Please don't shed a tear,
It's only that I love you
And need you by my side
I need you always in my life
My Love, my life, my guide.
You keep me safe, you keep me warm
You keep me well away from harm,
You'll always be beside me
I know we'll never part
The only one I'll ever love
The keeper of my heart.
And if one night you should awake
You see me lying there
The moonlight through the window
Shining on my hair
A little smile upon my face
A look of happiness
I must be dreaming of you
Nothing more or less.
You keep me safe, you keep me warm
You keep me well away from harm
You'll always be beside me
I know we'll never part
The only one I'll ever love
The keeper of my heart
And if one day you should awake
You find that I'm not there
Please don't let it worry you
Because you know I care
I won't be all that far away
My love is strong and true
No matter where I have to be
My love is just for you.
You keep me safe , you keep me warm
Protecting me from harm
We've been together many years
You know we'll never part
You'll be the only one who is :The keeper of my heart.

87. FOR YOU

I'm living for tomorrow
Living just for you
And every little thing I do
Is done with love for you.

Every little breath I take
And each beat of my heart
Will always just be done for you
Until the day we part.

I'm living for tomorrow
And loving only you
A love that's strong, a love that's true
A love that's just for you.

88. ON AND ON

There's just no getting over you
No matter what I say or do,
You're often in my memories
Often in my thoughts
Although the time may quickly go
There's no one who can really know
The pain I feel within my heart
Now that you are gone
The pain should heal in time I know
It seems to stay and will not go
I know I never will forget
The love of my dear Mother.

89. TELL ME

Tell me what you want my dear
To make you smile today
Tell me what your wish would be
You only have to say
I'd travel to the very end
Swim to farthest shore
Reach up for the brightest star
This and so much more.
You only have to tell me
What will make you smile
What will make you happy
For a little while
I'd climb the highest mountain
Even catch the moon
Tell me what it is my dear
But tell me very soon.
Tell me what you want my dear
To make me smile today
Just say you'll always love me
And beside me you will stay.

90. A NIGHT AT HOME

Sitting in my armchair
There's not a place to go
Sipping on a glass of wine
The lights are turned down low.
I look out of the window
There's not a soul in sight
But that may be because it is
The middle of the night.
I drink another glass of wine
The fire burns down low
I look out of the window
And watch the falling snow.
I look out from my armchair
The window starts to go
I drink another glass of wine
The bottle's getting low.
I look out of the bottle
Finish off the wine
And falling drunk onto the floor
My nose begins to shine.

91. DIVINE INTERVENTION?

Harry the hedgehog was sat in the grass
Waiting to cross the road
Watching the cars go rushing by
When one of them squashed a toad.
"Oh no" sighed Harry "Not again,
What are we going to do?
Everyday it's just the same
And someone that I knew."

Harry the hedgehog was sat in the grass
Hiding from the gale
The branches bending in the wind
And Harry heard a wail.
A car was braking very hard,
A tree fell to the ground,
Landing straight upon the car
With a crunching sound.

Harry the hedgehog was sat in the grass
A smile upon his face
And wondered how the driver felt
Put in Harry's place.
Squashed by something bigger
No chance to get away,
Just like Harry and his friends
Faced the same each day.

92. MEMORIES ARE MADE OF THIS 1.

Fluffy white clouds
Went floating by,
Familiar shapes
In a lovely blue sky,
One was a duck,
One was a boat,
One even looked like
An old overcoat.
Then running on down
To play by the stream,
Those long sunny days
Now seem like a dream.
Trees that looked greener
We'd climb every day,
Fields that we'd run through
Whilst farmers made hay.
Laughing out loud,
Having such fun,
It seems to me now
Those days are long gone.
Cold winter days
With ice and with snow,
Dark winter evenings
Where did they go?
Making a snowman
And making a slide,
Playing outdoors,
Never inside.

2.

We may have got wet
And shivered with cold,
But we always seemed happy
In those days of old.
Go carts we made
From old wheels and wood,
Racing each other
As fast as we could.
Games that we played,
Like hopscotch or tag,
Or even some fun
From an old straw filled bag.
We hadn't computers
Or video games,
Yet we filled our days
With fun just the same.
We didn't need TV
To keep us amused,
We just made our fun
From things that we used.
Cardboard and bottles
All kinds of strings,
We just made our fun
From these kinds of things.
Treehouses made
From bits of old wood,
Dams built on streams
Until they would flood.
Hunting for fossils
Picking wild flowers,
Things such as this
Kept us happy for hours.

3.
Going for walks
With mothers and friends,
Days like these
Never had ends.
Young and innocent,
Happiness, bliss,
Whatever happened
To things like this.
Making a swing
From a branch on a tree,
Sharing our sweets
One for you, one for me.
We didn't have worries
In days filled with fun,
Those were the days
Before life had begun.
I'd rather go back
To those days of before,
Life getting older
Can be such a bore.
We have to be sensible
Quiet and calm,
No acting fools
It might cause us harm.
Our childhood days
Are things we now miss,
But remember, our memories
Are made of this

93. MEMORIES ARE MADE OF THIS 2.

As we grow older
Some things we forget,
Like friends that we played with
Or people we met.
Then suddenly one day
Out of the blue,
A sound or a smell
Returns them to you.
Monday was washing
Friday was fish,
Also for baking
These things I miss.
Sunday was lunch
A family affair,
Roast beef and puds
With everyone there.
It seems to me now
That as we move on,
Family traditions
Are now long gone.
Out gathering firewood
Chopping up sticks,
Bringing in coal
A fire we'd fix.
At the end of the evening
The fire was low,
Toast would be done
On embers that glow.

2.

Sunday evenings
The radio on,
"Sing Something Simple"
Sang favourite songs.
Friday evenings
Was bingo and whist,
Down in the village hall
Nobody missed.
Thursdays was youthclub
With everyone there,
No argue or fighting
We knew how to share.
And then there was summer
A barn was cleaned out.
A dance would be held
A caller would shout,
"Take your partners,
Dosey Doe!"
The dance began
Off we'd go.
Whirling round
Moving on,
Changing partners
One by one.
We'd sit upon bales
Round the side of the barn,
Listening to old folk
Spinning a yarn.

3.

Those were the people
We saw every day,
They'd been there forever
They're still there today.
But when I go back
I find some are gone,
Dear old friends
Who have now passed on.
And where is the bogey man?
Where did he go?
It made us behave
In case he would show.
Where are the gypsies
With pegs and with heather?
Telling our fortunes
In all kinds of weather.
A garden party
Village fete,
Someone's at
The garden gate.
They're bringing me back
A sweet memory,
Of happy times
That used to be.
They're bringing me news
Of someone I miss,
Reminding me memories
Are made of this!

94. MEMORIES ARE MADE OF THIS 3.

Pat a cake, pat a cake
Bakers man
And rhymes such as this
Told by dear Gran.
Whilst grandfather sat
He rocked in his chair,
The smell of pipe smoke
Filling the air.
Grandma drank Milkmaid
Or Double D stout,
Always at home
She never drank out.
We'd go to the seaside
And play on the beach,
Or go for a paddle
But first they would preach.
"Take care as you paddle
Don't go too deep"
Then over the waves
We all would leap.
Holding hands
And splashing about,
Grandma and Grandad
And us would all shout.
Going back home
We'd travel by bus,
Sitting upstairs
Was a treat just for us.

2.

When we were with them
We had so much fun,
A tear fills my eye
When I think they're now gone.
With summer soon over
Autumn was here,
We went to get blackberries
Every year.
And into an orchard
We all would sneak,
To go pinching apples
Every week.
Sometimes we got caught
Or maybe just seen,
But still we went back
Again and again.
Peas from the pod
Tasted the best,
Pinched from the garden
Of old Mr S.
We never meant harm
By doing these things,
It didn't cause pain
That violence brings.
Sometimes we were good
And old folk we'd meet,
To say an "Hello"
And be given a sweet.

3.

Fireman's laces
Gobstoppers too,
And aniseed centre
Once you'd sucked through.
Lots of loose sweets
That you bought by the pound,
Lined up in jars
At the sweet shop you found.
Those were the days
Of long ago,
The village shop goods
Were all on show.
A chair by the counter
Where people could sit,
Chatting for hours
Or just for a bit.
We didn't have superstores
Way out of town,
But sometimes the grocer van
Would come around.
The baker with bread came
A "veggie" van too,
You didn't go shopping
It came to you.
It's all of these things
And much more that we miss,
So remember, our memories
Are made of this.

95. YOU

It's not a very lonely life
When you are around,
To feel your touch or see your smile
Or just to hold your hand.
I could not live without you
To have you by my side,
Sharing joy and beauty
You open my eyes wide.
You carry me in days of pain
When sorrow weighs me down,
You put a smile back on my face
When it wears a frown.
You say you always want me
To have me by your side,
And yet you seem to be the one
Who always is the guide.
My life would be quite empty
If you weren't around
Smiles and joy, love and life
With you, these things I've found.
There's really only one thing left
That I can find to say,
"Thank you" my sweet darling
You make my every day.

96. LEFT ALL ON HER OWN

She seemed so sad and lonely
As she was sitting there,
No one seemed to bother
No one seemed to care.
Sometimes it didn't matter
That she was all alone,
She'd please herself just what she did
When she was on her own.
But sometimes on a winters night
There's some things she would miss,
Loving arms to hold her,
Or someone just to kiss.
It always seemed like old age
Could really be a pain,
If only she could see her love
Just one more time again.
Taken from her long ago
And left all on her own,
Waiting for the day to come
When she too would be gone.

97. THAT SINKING FEELING

Down, down, I'm sinking
Who can save me now?
I find that there is no way out
And if there is,
                    Then how?
And then I start to slip away
I'm sinking further still,
My eyes begin to close on me
And then I lose my will.
I waken up with such a start
Many hours on,
Sleeping in my armchair
I find that daylight's gone.

98. (THE GREAT) ESCAPE

I sat upon my magic carpet
Went out for a ride,
The night was warm the sky was clear
As I flew outside.
Round the stars and past the moon
Beyond the Milky Way,
Upon my magic carpet
My cares soon fly away.
I visit lands beyond the stars
Find creatures strange and new,
Have some grand adventures
Each one strange but true.
Upon my magic carpet
I know that I will find,
Escape from all my daily chores
Far beyond my mind.

99. LUNCHTIME (REVENGE)

Little old lady sits in the park
Feeding ducks until it's dark,
Stands up, and walks away
Does the same most every day.
Comes back next day, bag of bread
Humming a tune going round in her head.
Breaks up crumbs and throws them down
Very soon the ducks swim round.
All day long just the same
Feeding ducks now almost tame.
Heavy rain starts falling down
Little old lady goes to town
Goes round shops buying bread
There's hungry ducks needing fed.
Little old lady, lots of money
Feeds the ducks which she thinks funny,
For when she dies and passes on
All her money will be gone,
From feeding ducks with lots of bread
No family fighting when she's dead.

100. Ben (Rockie or Magoulle – any one of you)

I've seen the face of an angel
Looking straight at me,
And felt a breath of heaven
Drifting aimlessly,
Beating in your chest
I hear a heart of gold,
And the love you give our way
Is very many fold,
You may not understand
All the things we say,
But you always seem to know
In your very own sweet way,
How can I put down in words
The feelings that I have,
A dog like you has captured
My heart, my soul, my Love.